Lotto in Italiano

A Fun Way to Reinforce Italian Vocabulary

Colette Elliott and Lia Mulholland

We hope you and your pupils enjoy playing the lotto games in this book. Brilliant Publications publishes many other books for teaching modern foreign languages. To find out more details on any of the titles listed below, please log onto our website: **www.brilliantpublications.co.uk**.

100+ Fun Ideas for Practising Modern Foreign Languages in the Primary Classroom	978-1-903853-98-6
More Fun Ideas for Advancing Modern Foreign Languages in the Primary Classroom	978-1-905780-72-3
Giochiamo Tutti Insieme	978-1-903853-96-2
Buon'Idea	978-1-905780-64-8
¡Es Español!	978-1-903853-64-1
Juguemos Todos Juntos	978-1-903853-95-5
¡Vamos a Cantar!	978-1-905780-13-6
Spanish Pen Pals Made Easy	978-1-905780-42-3
Spanish Festivals and Traditions	978-1-905780-53-2
Lotto en Español	978-1-905780-47-1
Buena Idea	978-1-905780-63-1
Chantez Plus Fort!	978-1-903853-37-5
Hexagonie 1	978-1-903853-92-4
Jouons Tous Ensemble	978-1-903853-81-8
C'est Français!	978-1-903853-02-3
J'aime Chanter!	978-1-905780-11-2
J'aime Parler!	978-1-905780-12-9
French Pen Pals Made Easy	978-1-905780-10-5
Loto Français	978-1-905780-47-1
French Festivals and Traditions	978-1-905780-44-0
Bonne Idée	978-1-905780-62-4
Unforgettable French	978-1-905780-54-9
Das ist Deutsch	978-1-905780-15-0
Wir Spielen Zusammen	978-1-903853-97-9
German Pen Pals Made Easy	978-1-905780-43-3
Deutsch-Lotto	978-1-905780-46-4
German Festivals and Traditions	978-1-905780-52-5
Gute Idee	978-1-905780-65-5

Published by Brilliant Publications
Unit 10
Sparrow Hall Farm
Edlesborough
Dunstable
Bedfordshire
LU6 2ES, UK

Sales and stock enquiries:
Tel: 01202 712910
Fax: 0845 1309300
E-mail: brilliant@bebc.co.uk
Website: www.brilliantpublications.co.uk

General information enquiries:
Tel: 01525 222292

The name Brilliant Publications and the logo are registered trademarks.

Written by Colette Elliott and Lia Mulholland
Illustrated by Gaynor Berry
Front cover designed by Brilliant Publications

© Text Colette Elliott and Lia Mulholland 2009
© Design Brilliant Publications 2009

Printed ISBN: 978-1-905780-48-8
ebook ISBN: 978-0-85747-117-8

First printed and published in the UK in 2009.
Reprinted 2010.
10 9 8 7 6 5 4 3 2

The right of Colette Elliott and Lia Mulholland to be identified as the authors of this work has been asserted by themselves in accordance with the Copyright, Designs and Patents Act 1988.

Pages 7–57 may be photocopied by individual teachers acting on behalf of the purchasing institution for classroom use only, without permission from the publisher and without declaration to the Publishers Licensing Society. The materials may not be reproduced in any other form or for any other purpose without the prior permission of the publisher.

Contents

Introduction 4
How to play 5
Different ways of playing/ideas 6

I numeri da 1 a 12 (Numbers 1–12)
        Call sheet 8
        Picture only boards 9–10
        Pictures and words boards 11–12
        Words only boards 13–14

I numeri da 1 a 60 (Numbers 1–60)
        Call sheet 15
        Picture only boards 16–17
        Pictures and words boards 18–19
        Words only boards 20–21

Gli animali (Animals)
        Call sheet 22
        Picture only boards 23–24
        Pictures and words boards 25–26
        Words only boards 27–28

Buon appetito! (Food)
        Call sheet 29
        Picture only boards 30–31
        Pictures and words boards 32–33
        Words only boards 34–35

In classe (Classroom objects)
        Call sheet 36
        Picture only boards 37–38
        Pictures and words boards 39–40
        Words only boards 41–42

I vestiti (Clothes)
        Call sheet 43
        Picture only boards 44–45
        Pictures and words boards 46–47
        Words only boards 48–49

Natale (Christmas)
        Call sheet 50
        Picture only boards 51–52
        Pictures and words boards 53–54
        Words only boards 55–56

Blank template boards 57
List of vocabulary used in games 58

Introduction

The perennially popular game of lotto is an enjoyable and effective way to teach and/or reinforce vocabulary and language structures. It can be used as a teaching tool or as a fun follow-up activity after a lesson. It provides a stimulating and meaningful way to develop reading, listening and speaking skills.

The games in *Lotto in Italiano* can be played in a variety of ways (see pages 5–7) and with very little preparation from you. There is no need to give the children counters or individual cards. Simply photocopy the boards, hand them out to your pupils together with some colouring pencils and, bingo, you can start playing!

Our unique call sheets provide the 'order of call' and enable you to follow the game closely and to select which team you want to win.

Lotto can be played in small groups, or with an entire class. There is no limit to the number of players and the games are suitable for ages four upwards.

There are seven topics in *Lotto in Italiano*:
- I numeri da 1 a 12   Numbers 1–12
- I numeri da 1 a 60   Numbers 1–60
- Gli animali   Animals
- Buon appetito!   Food
- In classe   Classroom objects
- I vestiti   Clothes
- Natale   Christmas

For each topic there are three versions of the boards, allowing maximum flexibility, particularly in mixed ability classes.

pictures only

words and pictures

words only

The ideas in this book are by no means exhaustive and, should you decide to cut the boards to make flashcards or playing cards, then the number of games is unlimited!

Have fun playing!

How to play

Getting started
For each topic, in each format, there are four different numbered boards, so you can play with four teams. Just photocopy the sheets, cut them in half, and hand out the boards to the children. For a class of 28 pupils, you only need to copy two pages seven times each.

It is a good idea to go through the vocabulary with the children before playing. The best way to do this is either to scan and place the four boards on the whiteboard, or enlarge the 12 pictures on the photocopier and use them as flashcards.

Make sure that the boards are evenly distributed throughout the class. After giving the boards out and before you start playing, ask for a show of hands to see how the teams are spread out in the classroom. The children like to see who is in their team and this increases the element of competition!

How to play
Each topic contains a call sheet, with the words numbered 1 to 12. The caller can start calling from any number. The white area in the table indicates who the winning board will be.

The children can play on their own or in pairs for moral support.

The winner is the first child to shout 'lotto' (hopefully the rest of that team will also shout 'lotto', but the real winner is the child who shouts out first). Get the winner to say all the words in Italian whilst you check on the list. This is a good reading/speaking exercise.

Once the first team has won, you can stop the game or carry on until everyone has shouted 'lotto' (you will know from the call sheet who the next winner will be).

You can play several games with the same boards by marking the boards in different ways:
- Colour the box outline (or only one side of the box if you want to make it last!)
- Colour the picture
- Colour the background
- Tick or cross the box, etc.

It is best to tell the children to shout 'lotto' as soon as the caller says the word, rather than wait until the colouring is done, as this may cause arguments amongst the children!

Variations
Instead of evenly distributing the boards, you could make it a competition within the class: divide the class into four groups, give the same boards to each group, and see which group says 'lotto' first.

Children could play in groups of five. One child is the caller (give him/her a photocopy of the call list) and the others use four different boards. Only one winner this time!

The order of call is the same for all the topics, so you can play 'mix and match' games with different topics. If you decide to do so, make sure that the four different teams are evenly spread.

Different ways of playing/ideas

- Call the words from the call sheet in Italian. Start anywhere, but make a note of where you started on a separate sheet of paper. Alternatively, get a child to do the calling. Assist him/her with the more difficult words.

- The children take it in turns to call out an item from their own board in Italian. When they call a word, they colour their own picture and everybody who has that picture says 'grazie' and colours their picture. Then the child sitting next to the caller says the next word, etc. This is a very good reading exercise if the 'words only' boards are used. The teacher should make a note of which items have been called on the call sheet.

- Call the words in English, and the children have to find the Italian translation (this can only be played with the 'words only' boards).

- Show a picture without saying anything (using the 'words only' boards).

- Write a word on the board without saying anything (for 'pictures only' boards).

- Instead of using the call sheets, photocopy the boards and cut them up into cards, then pick the cards out of a hat. The pupils could take turns to pick a card and call out the word.

- Ask the children to colour the pictures before playing and then call the words with a colour, eg "un gatto rosso". To keep the game from lasting too long, limit the children to the same two colours. (You can use the two columns on the call sheets to indicate the colour. For example, write B for "blu" at the top of the list of Italian words and R for "rosso" at the top of the English word list.)

- Give a description of the word in Italian.

- For the number "lotto" boards, give sums for the children to work out.

- Spell the words.

- Give a rhyming word.

- Include the word in a sentence eg una caramella; una caramella per piacere; vorrei una caramella per piacere; buogiorno signora, vorrei una caramella per piacere.

- . Make the game last the whole lesson. Give the boards at the beginning and call the words at intervals during the lesson, either on their own or in a sentence.

- Give everybody the same board. Each child has to preselect four items by circling or colouring them.

- Give the children the blank template board (pages 57) and get them to write/draw their own items/numbers from a list you have given on the board. This can be played with any topic/structures/verbs/grammar.

- ◆ Make the children repeat the word several times whilst they are colouring.
- ◆ The children ask each other a question each time, eg:

    - ✱ Che cos'hai?   What would you like?

    - ✱ Quanti? Che numero?   How many? What number?
      Cosa vuoi?   What would you like?

    - ✱ Che cos'e'?   What is this?

    - ✱ Cosa mangi?   What are you eating?

    - ✱ Hai un animale?   Do you have an animal/pets?

    - ✱ Che vestito porti?   What are you wearing?

- ◆ If you photocopy the boards double-sided, they will last even longer.

I numeri da 1 a 12

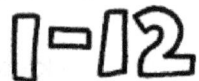

Team 1 to win	Start on 2 or 7
Team 2 to win	Start on 1, 3, 4 or 12
Team 3 to win	Start on 3, 5, 7, 10 or 11
Team 4 to win	Start on 5, 7, 8 or 9
All teams to win	Start on 6

These numbers refer to the numbers on the left and right of the grid below.

Tick the white boxes in the grid as you call out the words.

				Winning team										
				2	1	2&3	2	3&4	All	1,3,4	4	4	3	3	2	
	1	cinque	five													1
	2	nove	nine													2
	3	undici	eleven													3
	4	due	two													4
	5	quattro	four													5
	6	dodici	twelve													6
	7	tre	three													7
	8	uno	one													8
	9	sei	six													9
Order of call	10	otto	eight													10
	11	dieci	ten													11
	12	sette	seven													12
	1	cinque	five													1
	2	nove	nine													2
	3	undici	eleven													3
	4	due	two													4
	5	quattro	four													5
	6	dodici	twelve													6
	7	tre	three													7
	8	uno	one													8
	9	sei	six													9

Lotto! (Squadra 1)   Nome: _____   1-12

| 2 | 8 | 9 |
| 3 | 1 | 4 |

Lotto in Italiano – I numeri da 1 a 12

© Colette Elliott, Lia Mulholland and Brilliant Publications.
This board may be photocopied for use by the purchaser.

Lotto! (Squadra 2)   Nome: _____   1-12

| 1 | 5 | 6 |
| 4 | 12 | 2 |

Lotto in Italiano – I numeri da 1 a 12

© Colette Elliott, Lia Mulholland and Brilliant Publications.
This board may be photocopied for use by the purchaser.

Lotto! (Squadra 3)   Nome: _____   1-12

7	5	10
11	3	4

Lotto in Italiano – I numeri da 1 a 12   © *Colette Elliott, Lia Mulholland and Brilliant Publications.*
This board may be photocopied for use by the purchaser.

Lotto! (Squadra 4)   Nome: _____   1-12

11	4	6
7	8	9

Lotto in Italiano – I numeri da 1 a 12   © *Colette Elliott, Lia Mulholland and Brilliant Publications.*
This board may be photocopied for use by the purchaser.

Lotto! (Squadra 1) Nome: _____ 1-12

2 due	8 otto	9 nove
3 tre	1 uno	4 quattro

Lotto in Italiano – I numeri da 1 a 12

© Colette Elliott, Lia Mulholland and Brilliant Publications.
This board may be photocopied for use by the purchaser.

Lotto! (Squadra 2) Nome: _____ 1-12

1 uno	5 cinque	6 sei
4 quattro	12 dodici	2 due

Lotto in Italiano – I numeri da 1 a 12

© Colette Elliott, Lia Mulholland and Brilliant Publications.
This board may be photocopied for use by the purchaser.

Lotto! (Squadra 3) Nome: _____ 1-12

7 sette	5 cinque	10 dieci
11 undici	3 tre	4 quattro

Lotto! (Squadra 4) Nome: _____ 1-12

11 undici	4 quattro	6 sei
7 sette	8 otto	9 nove

Lotto! (Squadra 1) Nome: _____ 1-12

due	otto	nove
tre	uno	quattro

Lotto in Italiano – I numeri da 1 a 12

© *Colette Elliott, Lia Mulholland and Brilliant Publications.*
This board may be photocopied for use by the purchaser.

Lotto! (Squadra 2) Nome: _____ 1-12

uno	cinque	sei
quattro	dodici	due

Lotto in Italiano – I numeri da 1 a 12

© *Colette Elliott, Lia Mulholland and Brilliant Publications.*
This board may be photocopied for use by the purchaser.

Lotto! (Squadra 3) Nome: _____ 1-12

sette	cinque	dieci
undici	tre	quattro

Lotto in Italiano – I numeri da 1 a 12

© Colette Elliott, Lia Mulholland and Brilliant Publications.
This board may be photocopied for use by the purchaser.

Lotto! (Squadra 4) Nome: _____ 1-12

undici	quattro	sei
sette	otto	nove

Lotto in Italiano – I numeri da 1 a 12

© Colette Elliott, Lia Mulholland and Brilliant Publications.
This board may be photocopied for use by the purchaser.

I numeri da 1 a 60

Team 1 to win	Start on 2 or 7
Team 2 to win	Start on 1, 3, 4 or 12
Team 3 to win	Start on 3, 5, 7, 10 or 11
Team 4 to win	Start on 5, 7, 8 or 9
All teams to win	Start on 6

These numbers refer to the numbers on the left and right of the grid below.

Tick the white boxes in the grid as you call out the words.

				Winning team										
				2	1	2&3	2	3&4	All	1,3,4	4	4	3	3	2	
	1	ventisei	twenty-six													1
	2	sette	seven													2
	3	sessanta	sixty													3
	4	trentacinque	thirty-five													4
	5	cinquantotto	fifty-eight													5
	6	quarantuno	forty-one													6
	7	quindici	fifteen													7
	8	cinquanta	fifty													8
Order of call	9	dodici	twelve													9
	10	quarantadue	forty-two													10
	11	trentaquattro	thirty-four													11
	12	diciannove	nineteen													12
	1	ventisei	twenty-six													1
	2	sette	seven													2
	3	sessanta	sixty													3
	4	trentacinque	thirty-five													4
	5	cinquantotto	fifty-eight													5
	6	quarantuno	forty-one													6
	7	quindici	fifteen													7
	8	cinquanta	fifty													8
	9	dodici	twelve													9

Lotto in Italiano

Lotto! (Squadra 1)   Nome: _____   1-60

35	42	7
15	50	58

Lotto in Italiano – I numeri da 1 a 60

© Colette Elliott, Lia Mulholland and Brilliant Publications.
This board may be photocopied for use by the purchaser.

Lotto! (Squadra 2)   Nome: _____   1-60

50	26	12
58	41	35

Lotto in Italiano – I numeri da 1 a 60

© Colette Elliott, Lia Mulholland and Brilliant Publications.
This board may be photocopied for use by the purchaser.

Lotto! (Squadra 3) Nome: _____ 1-60

19	26	34
60	15	58

Lotto in Italiano – I numeri da 1 a 60

© Colette Elliott, Lia Mulholland and Brilliant Publications.
This board may be photocopied for use by the purchaser.

Lotto! (Squadra 4) Nome: _____ 1-60

60	58	12
19	42	7

¡Lotto! (Squadra 1) Nome: _____   1-60

35 trentacinque	**42** quarantadue	**7** sette
15 quindici	**50** cinquanta	**58** cinquantotto

Lotto in Italiano – I numeri da 1 a 60

© Colette Elliott, Lia Mulholland and Brilliant Publications.
This board may be photocopied for use by the purchaser.

¡Lotto! (Squadra 2) Nome: _____   1-60

50 cinquanta	**26** ventisei	**12** dodici
58 cinquantotto	**41** quarantuno	**35** trentacinque

Lotto in Italiano – I numeri da 1 a 60

© Colette Elliott, Lia Mulholland and Brilliant Publications.
This board may be photocopied for use by the purchaser.

Lotto! (Squadra 3)   Nome: _____   1-60

19 diciannove	26 ventisei	34 trentaquattro
60 sessanta	15 quindici	58 cinquantotto

Lotto in Italiano – I numeri da 1 a 60

© Colette Elliott, Lia Mulholland and Brilliant Publications.
This board may be photocopied for use by the purchaser.

Lotto! (Squadra 4)   Nome: _____   1-60

60 sessanta	58 cinquantotto	12 dodici
19 diciannove	42 quarantadue	7 sette

Lotto in Italiano – I numeri da 1 a 60

© Colette Elliott, Lia Mulholland and Brilliant Publications.
This board may be photocopied for use by the purchaser.

Lotto! (Squadra 1) Nome: _____ 1-60

trentacinque	quarantadue	sette
quindici	cinquanta	cinquantotto

Lotto in Italiano – I numeri da 1 a 60

Lotto! (Squadra 2) Nome: _____ 1-60

cinquanta	ventisei	dodici
cinquantotto	quarantuno	trentacinque

Lotto! (Squadra 3) Nome: _____ 1-60

diciannove	ventisei	trentaquattro
sessanta	quindici	cinquantotto

Lotto! (Squadra 4) Nome: _____ 1-60

sessanta	cinquantotto	dodici
diciannove	quarantadue	sette

Gli animali

Team 1 to win	Start on 2 or 7
Team 2 to win	Start on 1, 3, 4 or 12
Team 3 to win	Start on 3, 5, 7, 10 or 11
Team 4 to win	Start on 5, 7, 8 or 9
All teams to win	Start on 6

These numbers refer to the numbers on the left and right of the grid below.

Tick the white boxes in the grid as you call out the words.

				Winning team											
				2	1	2&3	2	3&4	All	1,3,4	4	4	3	3	2	
Order of call	1	un porcello	a pig													1
	2	un topolino	a mouse													2
	3	una porcellino d'india	a guinea pig													3
	4	una mucca	a cow													4
	5	un criceto	a hamster													5
	6	un cavallo	a horse													6
	7	un coniglio	a rabbit													7
	8	un gatto	a cat													8
	9	un cane	a dog													9
	10	un pesce rosso	a goldfish													10
	11	un'anatra	a duck													11
	12	una gallina	a hen													12
	1	un porcello	a pig													1
	2	un topolino	a mouse													2
	3	un porcellino d'india	a guinea pig													3
	4	una mucca	a cow													4
	5	un criceto	a hamster													5
	6	un cavallo	a horse													6
	7	un coniglio	a rabbit													7
	8	un gatto	a cat													8
	9	un cane	a dog													9

Lotto! (Squadra 1)   Nome: _____

Lotto in Italiano – Gli animali

© Colette Elliott, Lia Mulholland and Brilliant Publications.
This board may be photocopied for use by the purchaser.

Lotto! (Squadra 2)   Nome: _____

Lotto in Italiano – Gli animali

© Colette Elliott, Lia Mulholland and Brilliant Publications.
This board may be photocopied for use by the purchaser.

Lotto! (Squadra 3)   Nome: _____

Lotto in Italiano – Gli animali

© Colette Elliott, Lia Mulholland and Brilliant Publications.
This board may be photocopied for use by the purchaser.

Lotto! (Squadra 4)   Nome: _____

Lotto in Italiano – Gli animali

© Colette Elliott, Lia Mulholland and Brilliant Publications.
This board may be photocopied for use by the purchaser.

Lotto! (Squadra 1)   Nome: _____

una mucca	un pesce rosso	un topolino

un coniglio	un gatto	un criceto

Lotto in Italiano – Gli animali

Lotto! (Squadra 2)   Nome: _____

un gatto	un porcello	un cane

un criceto	un cavallo	una mucca

Lotto in Italiano – Gli animali

Lotto! (Squadra 3)   Nome: _____

 una gallina	 un porcello	 un'anatra
 un porcellino d'india	 un coniglio	 un criceto

Lotto in Italiano – Gli animali

© Colette Elliott, Lia Mulholland and Brilliant Publications.
This board may be photocopied for use by the purchaser.

Lotto! (Squadra 4)   Nome: _____

 un porcellino d'india	 un criceto	 un cane
 una gallina	 un pesce rosso	 un topolino

Lotto in Italiano – Gli animali

© Colette Elliott, Lia Mulholland and Brilliant Publications.
This board may be photocopied for use by the purchaser.

Lotto! (Squadra 1) Nome: _____

una mucca	un pesce rosso	un topolino
un coniglio	un gatto	un criceto

Lotto in Italiano – Gli animali

Lotto! (Squadra 2) Nome: _____

un gatto	un porcello	un cane
un criceto	un cavallo	una mucca

Lotto in Italiano – Gli animali

Lotto! (Squadra 3) Nome: _____

una gallina	un porcello	un'anatra
un porcellino d'india	un coniglio	un criceto

Lotto in Italiano – Gli animali

Lotto! (Squadra 4) Nome: _____

un porcellino d'india	un criceto	un cane
una gallina	un pesce rosso	un topolino

Buon appetito!

Team 1 to win	Start on 2 or 7
Team 2 to win	Start on 1, 3, 4 or 12
Team 3 to win	Start on 3, 5, 7, 10 or 11
Team 4 to win	Start on 5, 7, 8 or 9
All teams to win	Start on 6

These numbers refer to the numbers on the left and right of the grid below.

Tick the white boxes in the grid as you call out the words.

					Winning team											
					2	1	2&3	2	3&4	All	1,3,4	4	4	3	3	2
Order of call	1	un dolce	a cake														1
	2	una mela	an apple														2
	3	un gelato	an ice-cream														3
	4	del formaggio	(some) cheese														4
	5	un pollo	a chicken														5
	6	una patata	a potato														6
	7	del latte	(some) milk														7
	8	del prosciutto	(some) ham														8
	9	un uovo	an egg														9
	10	delle patatine	(some) chips														10
	11	del pane	(some) bread														11
	12	delle caramelle	(some) sweets														12
	1	un dolce	a cake														1
	2	una mela	an apple														2
	3	un gelato	an ice-cream														3
	4	del formaggio	(some) cheese														4
	5	un pollo	a chicken														5
	6	una patata	a potato														6
	7	del latte	(some) milk														7
	8	del prosciutto	a ham														8
	9	un uovo	an egg														9

Lotto in Italiano

Lotto! (Squadra 1)   Nome: _____

 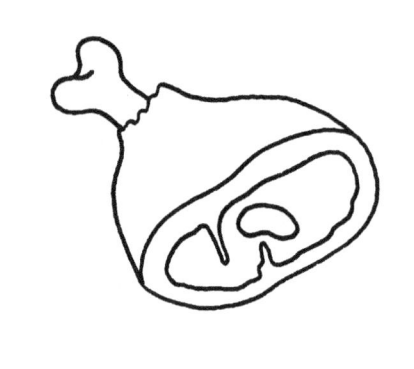 

Lotto in Italiano – Buon appetito!

Lotto! (Squadra 2)   Nome: _____

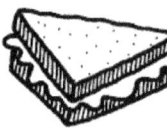

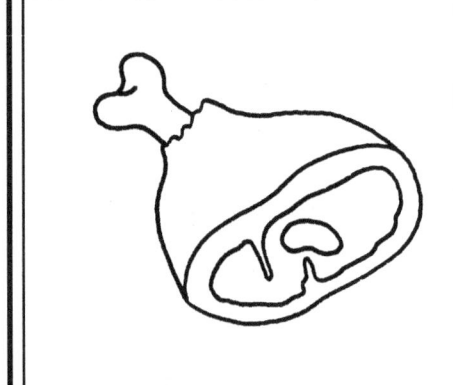  

Lotto in Italiano – Buon appetito!

Lotto! (Squadra 3)   Nome: _____

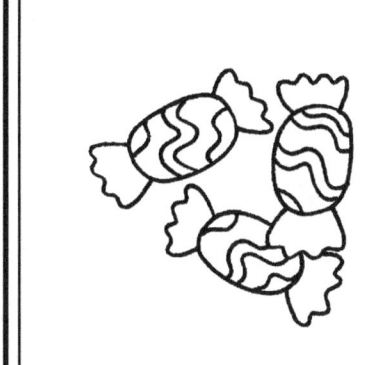  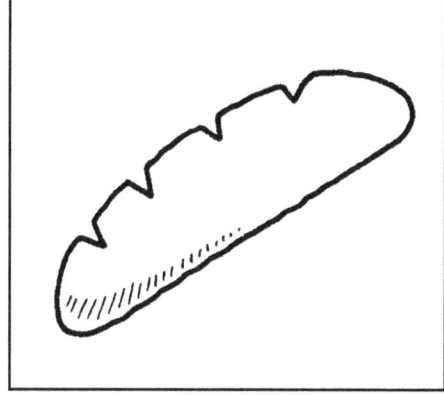

Lotto in Italiano – Buon appetito!

Lotto! (Squadra 4)   Nome: _____

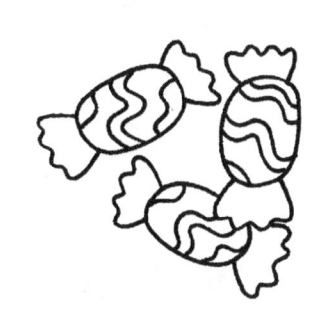  

Lotto in Italiano – Buon appetito!

Lotto! (Squadra 1)   Nome: _____

del formaggio	delle patatine	una mela
	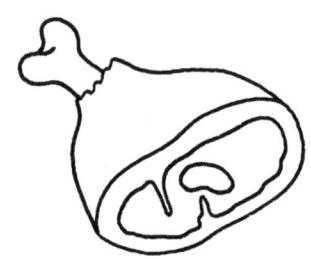	
del latte	del prosciutto	un pollo

Lotto! (Squadra 2)   Nome: _____

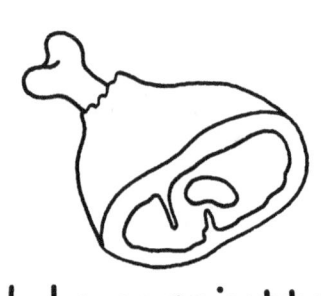		
del prosciutto	un dolce	un uovo
	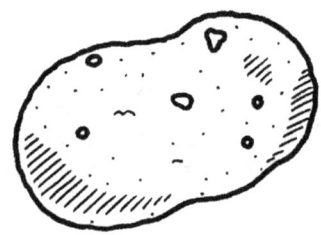	
un pollo	una patata	del formaggio

Lotto! (Squadra 3)   Nome: _____

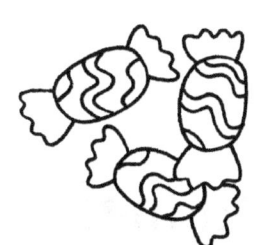
delle caramelle

un dolce

del pane

un gelato

del latte

un pollo

Lotto! (Squadra 4)   Nome: _____

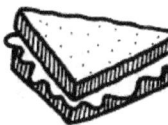

un gelato

un pollo

un uovo

delle caramelle

delle patatine

una mela

Lotto! (Squadra 1)   Nome: _____

del formaggio	delle patatine	una mela
del latte	del prosciutto	un pollo

Lotto in Italiano – Buon appetito! © Colette Elliott, Lia Mulholland and Brilliant Publications.
This board may be photocopied for use by the purchaser.

Lotto! (Squadra 2)   Nome: _____

del prosciutto	un dolce	un uovo
un pollo	una patata	del formaggio

Lotto in Italiano – Buon appetito! © Colette Elliott, Lia Mulholland and Brilliant Publications.
This board may be photocopied for use by the purchaser.

Lotto! (Squadra 3)   Nome: _____

delle caramelle	un dolce	del pane
un gelato	del latte	un pollo

Lotto in Italiano – Buon appetito!

Lotto! (Squadra 4)   Nome: _____

un gelato	un pollo	un uovo
delle caramelle	delle patatine	una mela

Lotto in Italiano – Buon appetito!

In classe

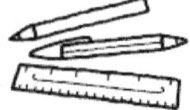

Team 1 to win	Start on 2 or 7
Team 2 to win	Start on 1, 3, 4 or 12
Team 3 to win	Start on 3, 5, 7, 10 or 11
Team 4 to win	Start on 5, 7, 8 or 9
All teams to win	Start on 6

These numbers refer to the numbers on the left and right of the grid below.

Tick the white boxes in the grid as you call out the words.

				Winning team										
				2	1	2&3	2	3&4	All	1,3,4	4	4	3	3	2	
Order of call	1	un libro	a book													1
	2	un temperamatite	a pencil sharpener													2
	3	un righello	a ruler													3
	4	una cartella	a school bag													4
	5	delle forbici	(some) scissors													5
	6	una matita	a pencil													6
	7	una gomma	a rubber													7
	8	un quaderno	an exercise book													8
	9	una penna	a pen													9
	10	un astuccio	a pencil case													10
	11	una calcolatrice	a calculator													11
	12	un bastoncino di colla	a glue stick													12
	1	un libro	a book													1
	2	un temperamatite	a pencil sharpener													2
	3	un righello	a ruler													3
	4	una cartella	a school bag													4
	5	delle forbici	(some) scissors													5
	6	un matita	a pencil													6
	7	une gomma	a rubber													7
	8	un quaderno	an exercise book													8
	9	una penna	a pen													9

Lotto! (Squadra 1)   Nome: _____

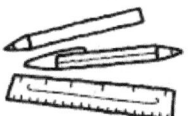

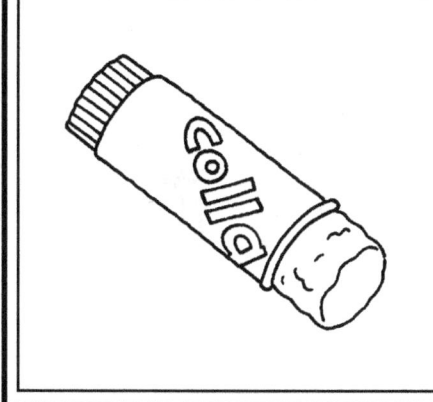

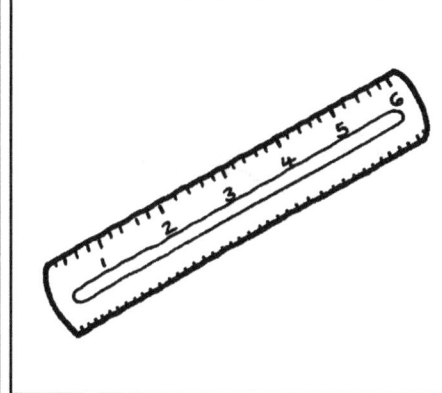

Lotto in Italiano – In classe

© Colette Elliott, Lia Mulholland and Brilliant Publications.
This board may be photocopied for use by the purchaser.

Lotto! (Squadra 2)   Nome: _____

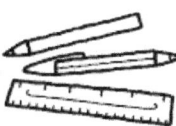

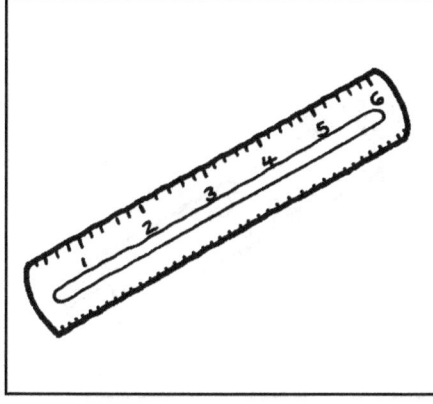

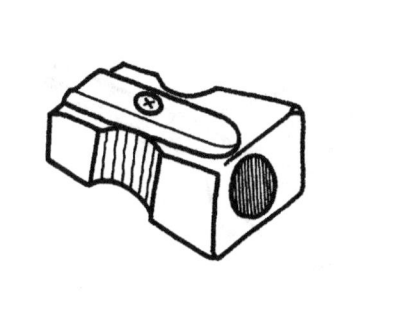

Lotto in Italiano – In classe

© Colette Elliott, Lia Mulholland and Brilliant Publications.
This board may be photocopied for use by the purchaser.

Lotto! (Squadra 3)   Nome: _____

  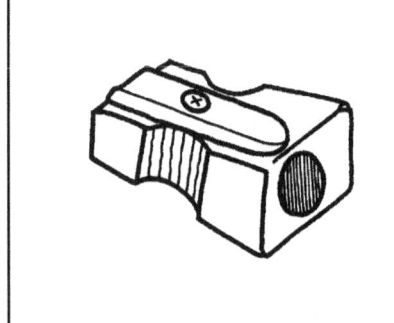

 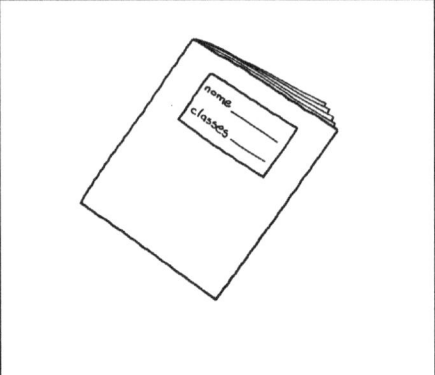 

Lotto in Italiano – In classe

© Colette Elliott, Lia Mulholland and Brilliant Publications.
This board may be photocopied for use by the purchaser.

Lotto! (Squadra 4)   Nome: _____

Lotto in Italiano – In classe

© Colette Elliott, Lia Mulholland and Brilliant Publications.
This board may be photocopied for use by the purchaser.

Lotto! (Squadra 1)   Nome: _____

un bastoncino di colla	un libro	una calcolatrice
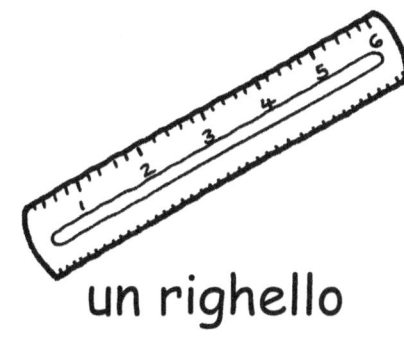		
un righello	una gomma	delle forbici

Lotto in Italiano – In classe

© Colette Elliott, Lia Mulholland and Brilliant Publications.
This board may be photocopied for use by the purchaser.

Lotto! (Squadra 2)   Nome: _____

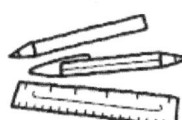

un righello	delle forbici	una penna
		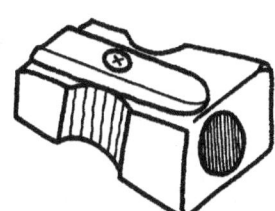
un bastoncino di colla	un astuccio	un tempera matite

Lotto in Italiano – In classe

© Colette Elliott, Lia Mulholland and Brilliant Publications.
This board may be photocopied for use by the purchaser.

Lotto! (Squadra 3)   Nome: _____

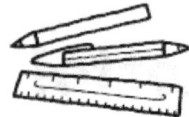

	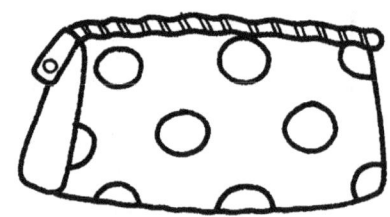	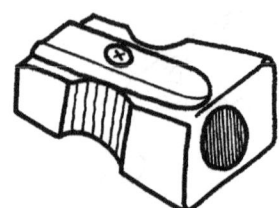
una cartella	un astuccio	un tempera matite

una gomma	un quaderno	delle forbici

Lotto in Italiano – In classe

© Colette Elliott, Lia Mulholland and Brilliant Publications.
This board may be photocopied for use by the purchaser.

Lotto! (Squadra 4)   Nome: _____

un quaderno	un libro	una penna

delle forbici	una matita	una cartella

© Colette Elliott, Lia Mulholland and Brilliant Publications.
This board may be photocopied for use by the purchaser.

Lotto! (Squadra 1) Nome: _____

un bastoncino di colla	un libro	una calcolatrice
un righello	una gomma	delle forbici

Lotto in Italiano – In classe

© Colette Elliott, Lia Mulholland and Brilliant Publications.
This board may be photocopied for use by the purchaser.

Lotto! (Squadra 2) Nome: _____

un righello	delle forbici	una penna
un bastoncino di colla	un astuccio	un tempera matite

Lotto in Italiano – In classe

© Colette Elliott, Lia Mulholland and Brilliant Publications.
This board may be photocopied for use by the purchaser.

Lotto! (Squadra 3) Nome: _____

una cartella	un astuccio	un tempera matite
una gomma	un quaderno	delle forbici

Lotto! (Squadra 4) Nome: _____

un quaderno	un libro	una penna
delle forbici	una matita	una cartella

I vestiti

Team 1 to win	Start on 2 or 7
Team 2 to win	Start on 1, 3, 4 or 12
Team 3 to win	Start on 3, 5, 7, 10 or 11
Team 4 to win	Start on 5, 7, 8 or 9
All teams to win	Start on 6

These numbers refer to the numbers on the left and right of the grid below.

Tick the white boxes in the grid as you call out the words.

				Winning team												
				2	1	2&3	2	3&4	All	1,3,4	4	4	3	3	2	
Order of call	1	delle scarpe	(some) shoes													1
	2	un maglione	a jumper													2
	3	un vestito	a dress													3
	4	i pantaloni	(a pair of) trousers													4
	5	i jeans	(a pair of) jeans													5
	6	una maglietta	a T-shirt													6
	7	un cappello	a hat													7
	8	una gonna	a skirt													8
	9	una camicia	a shirt													9
	10	una cravatta	a tie													10
	11	delle calze	(some) socks													11
	12	i pantaloncini	(a pair of) shorts													12
	1	delle scarpe	(some) shoes													1
	2	un maglione	a jumper													2
	3	un vestito	a dress													3
	4	i pantaloni	(a pair of) trousers													4
	5	i jeans	(a pair of) jeans													5
	6	una maglietta	a T-shirt													6
	7	un cappello	a hat													7
	8	una gonna	a skirt													8
	9	una camicia	a shirt													9

Lotto in Italiano

Lotto! (Squadra 1)   Nome: _____

Lotto in Italiano – I vestiti

© Colette Elliott, Lia Mulholland and Brilliant Publications.
This board may be photocopied for use by the purchaser.

Lotto! (Squadra 2)   Nome: _____

Lotto in Italiano – I vestiti

© Colette Elliott, Lia Mulholland and Brilliant Publications.
This board may be photocopied for use by the purchaser.

Lotto! (Squadra 3) Nome: _____

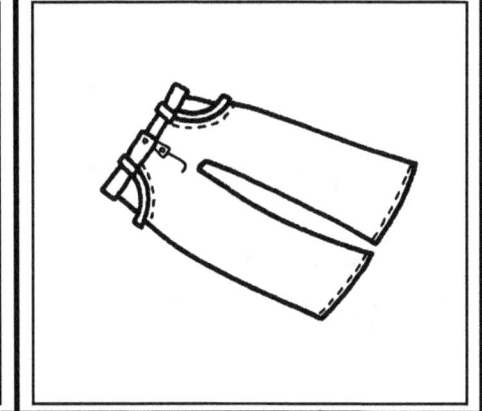

Lotto in Italiano – I vestiti

© Colette Elliott, Lia Mulholland and Brilliant Publications.
This board may be photocopied for use by the purchaser.

Lotto! (Squadra 4) Nome: _____

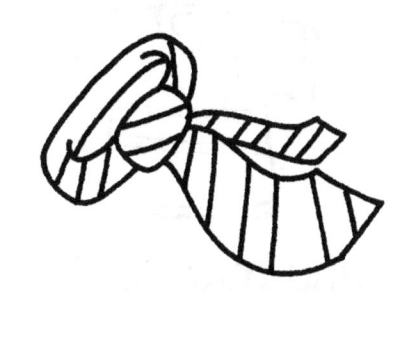

Lotto in Italiano – I vestiti

© Colette Elliott, Lia Mulholland and Brilliant Publications.
This board may be photocopied for use by the purchaser.

Lotto! (Squadra 1)   Nome: _____

	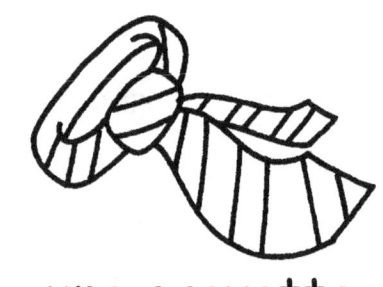	
i pantaloni	una cravatta	un maglione
		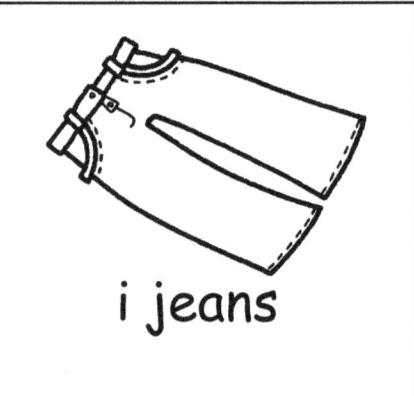
un cappello	una gonna	i jeans

Lotto in Italiano – I vestiti

© Colette Elliott, Lia Mulholland and Brilliant Publications.
This board may be photocopied for use by the purchaser.

Lotto! (Squadra 2)   Nome: _____

una gonna	delle scarpe	una camicia

i jeans	una maglietta	i pantaloni

Lotto! (Squadra 3)   Nome: _____

i pantaloncini	delle scarpe	delle calze

un vestito	un cappello	i jeans

Lotto in Italiano – I vestiti

Lotto! (Squadra 4)   Nome: _____

	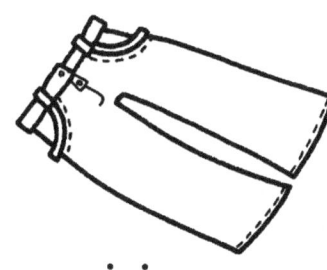	
un vestito	i jeans	una camicia
	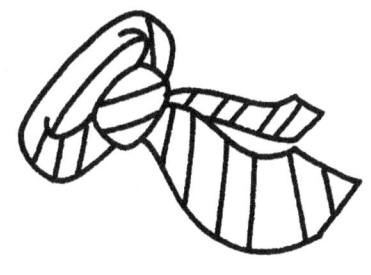	
i pantaloncini	una cravatta	un maglione

Lotto! (Squadra 1)   Nome: _____

i pantaloni	una cravatta	un maglione
un cappello	una gonna	i jeans

Lotto in Italiano – I vestiti

© Colette Elliott, Lia Mulholland and Brilliant Publications.
This board may be photocopied for use by the purchaser.

Lotto! (Squadra 2)   Nome: _____

una gonna	delle scarpe	una camicia
i jeans	una maglietta	i pantaloni

Lotto in Italiano – I vestiti

© Colette Elliott, Lia Mulholland and Brilliant Publications.
This board may be photocopied for use by the purchaser.

Lotto! (Squadra 3)   Nome: _____

i pantaloncini	delle scarpe	delle calze
un vestito	un cappello	i jeans

Lotto in Italiano – I vestiti

Lotto! (Squadra 4)   Nome: _____

un vestito	i jeans	una camicia
i pantaloncini	una cravatta	un maglione

Lotto in Italiano – I vestiti

Natale

Team 1 to win	Start on 2 or 7
Team 2 to win	Start on 1, 3, 4 or 12
Team 3 to win	Start on 3, 5, 7, 10 or 11
Team 4 to win	Start on 5, 7, 8 or 9
All teams to win	Start on 6

These numbers refer to the numbers on the left and right of the grid below.

Tick the white boxes in the grid as you call out the words.

				Winning team											
				2	1	2&3	2	3&4	All	1,3,4	4	4	3	3	2	
Order of call	1	il pungitopo	holly													1
	2	il tacchimo	the turkey													2
	3	Babbo Natale	Father Christmas													3
	4	il pupazzo di neve	the snowman													4
	5	Buon Natale!	Happy Christmas!													5
	6	l'albero di Natale	the Christmas tree													6
	7	il 25 dicembre	25th December													7
	8	la stella	the star													8
	9	i regali	the presents													9
	10	il presepe	the crib													10
	11	la candela	the candle													11
	12	la renna	a reindeer													12
	1	il pungitopo	holly													1
	2	il tacchimo	the turkey													2
	3	Babbo Natale	Father Christmas													3
	4	il pupazzo di neve	the snowman													4
	5	Buon Natale!	Happy Christmas!													5
	6	l'albero di Natale	the Christmas tree													6
	7	il 25 dicembre	25th December													7
	8	la stella	the star													8
	9	i regali	the presents													9

We have used the definite article (il/la) for the Christmas words (instead of the indefinite article as used for other topics) as it seemed more appropriate. This could provide the stimulus for getting children to practise both forms.

Lotto! (Squadra 1)   Nome: _____

Lotto in Italiano – Natale

© Colette Elliott, Lia Mulholland and Brilliant Publications.
This board may be photocopied for use by the purchaser.

Lotto! (Squadra 2)   Nome: _____

Lotto in Italiano – Natale

© Colette Elliott, Lia Mulholland and Brilliant Publications.
This board may be photocopied for use by the purchaser.

Lotto! (Squadra 3)   Nome: _____

Lotto in Italiano – Natale

© Colette Elliott, Lia Mulholland and Brilliant Publications.
This board may be photocopied for use by the purchaser.

Lotto! (Squadra 4)   Nome: _____

Lotto in Italiano – Natale

Lotto! (Squadra 1)   Nome: _____

il pupazzo di neve	il presepe	il tacchimo

il 25 dicembre	la stella	Buon Natale!

Lotto in Italiano – Natale

© Colette Elliott, Lia Mulholland and Brilliant Publications.
This board may be photocopied for use by the purchaser.

Lotto! (Squadra 2)   Nome: _____

la stella	il pungitopo	i regali

Buon Natale!	l'albero di Natale	il pupazzo di neve

Lotto in Italiano – Natale

Lotto! (Squadra 3)   Nome: _____

la renna	il pungitopo	la candela

Babbo Natale	il 25 dicembre	

Lotto in Italiano – Natale

Lotto! (Squadra 4)   Nome: _____

Babbo Natale		i regali

la renna	il presepe	il tacchimo

Lotto! (Squadra 1)   Nome: _____

il pupazzo di neve	il presepe	il tacchimo
il 25 dicembre	la stella	Buon Natale!

Lotto in Italiano – Natale

Lotto! (Squadra 2)   Nome: _____

la stella	il pungitopo	il regali
Buon Natale!	l'albero di Natale	il pupazzo di neve

Lotto! (Squadra 3) Nome: _____

la renna	il pungitopo	la candela
Babbo Natale	il 25 dicembre	Buon Natale!

Lotto! (Squadra 4) Nome: _____

Babbo Natale	Buon Natale!	i regali
la renna	il presepe	il tacchimo

Lotto! (Squadra   )   Nome: _____

Lotto in Italiano

© Colette Elliott, Lia Mulholland and Brilliant Publications.
This board may be photocopied for use by the purchaser.

Lotto! (Squadra   )   Nome: _____

List of vocabulary used in the games

I numeri da 1 a 12
uno	1
due	2
tre	3
quattro	4
cinque	5
sei	6
sette	7
otto	8
nove	9
dieci	10
undici	11
dodici	12

I numeri da 1 a 60
sette	7
dodici	12
quindici	15
diciannove	19
ventisei	26
trentaquattro	34
trentacinque	35
quarantuno	41
quarantadue	42
cinquanta	50
cinquantotto	58
sessanta	60

Gli animali
un'anatra	a duck
un gatto	a cat
un cavallo	a horse
un cane	a dog
un porcello	a pig
un porcellino d'india	a Guinea pig
un criceto	a hamster
un coniglio	a rabbit
un pesce rosso	a goldfish
una gallina	a hen
un topolino	a mouse
una mucca	a cow

Buon appetito!
delle caramelle	(some) sweets
delle patatine	(some) chips
del formaggio	(some) cheese
un dolce	a cake
un gelato	an ice-cream
un uovo	an egg
del pane	(some) bread
un pollo	a chicken
una mela	an apple
del prosciutto	(some) ham
una patata	a potato
del latte	a carton of milk

In classe
un bastoncino di colla	a glue stick
un quaderno	an exercise book
una calcolatrice	a calculator
una cartella	a school bag
delle forbici	(some) scissors
una matita	a pencil
una gomma	a rubber
un libro	a book
un righello	a ruler
una penna	a pen
un tempera matite	a pencil sharpener
un astuccio	a pencil case

I vestiti
un cappello	a hat
delle calze	(some) socks
delle scarpe	(some) shoes
una camicia	a shirt
una cravatta	a tie
i jeans	(a pair of) jeans
un vestito	a dress
i pantaloni	(a pair of) trousers
un maglione	a jumper
una gonna	a skirt
i pantaloncini	a pair of shorts
una maglietta	a T-shirt

Natale
il pungitopo	holly
il tacchimo	the turkey
Babbo Natale	Father Christmas
Buon Natale!	Happy Christmas!
l'albero di Natale	the Christmas tree
il 25 dicembre	25th December
la stella	the star
i regali	the presents
il presepe	the crib
la candela	the candle
la renna	the reindeer
il pupazzo di neve	the snowman